LITTLE KIDS
FIRST
BIG
BOOK OF THE
OCEAN

CATHERINE D. HUGHES

LITTLE KIDS FIRST BIG BOOK OF THE OCEAN

CATHERINE D. HUGHES

NATIONAL GEOGRAPHIC KIDS

WASHINGTON, D.C.

CONTENTS

INTRODUCTION

This book introduces Earth's ocean and explores it through the animals that live there. It answers questions from "What is the ocean?" and "Why are there waves?" to "Which animals live in the ocean?" and "How do whales breathe?"

Seen from space, Earth looks like a big blue marble. Almost three-quarters of the planet is covered by one big ocean. Parts of this one, single ocean have been given names: Pacific Ocean, Atlantic Ocean, Indian Ocean, and Arctic Ocean. All of the parts are interconnected. A map at the back of the book shows where each part of the ocean is located.

NATIONAL GEOGRAPHIC KIDS FIRST BIG BOOK OF THE OCEAN IS DIVIDED INTO FOUR CHAPTERS:

CHAPTER 3
INDIAN OCEAN
The Indian Ocean is the third largest ocean. It formed about 65 million years ago, making it the youngest ocean.

CHAPTER THREE

brings the reader to the Indian Ocean, tucked below Asia and between Africa and Australia. The animals highlighted here are sea creatures typically found in this part of the vast ocean.

CHAPTER 1
PACIFIC OCEAN
The biggest part of Earth's ocean is called the Pacific Ocean. In this chapter you will meet a few of the animals that live there.

CHAPTER 2
ATLANTIC OCEAN
The second biggest part of the ocean is the Atlantic. It is also the saltiest. Let's take a look at a few animals you might see there.

CHAPTER 4
ARCTIC OCEAN
The Arctic Ocean is the smallest and coldest ocean.

CHAPTER ONE

begins the book with a look at the animals you can find in the largest part of the ocean, the Pacific. The deepest place on Earth is in the Pacific Ocean: the Challenger Deep in the Mariana Trench.

CHAPTER TWO

continues the exploration of the ocean and its inhabitants with a visit to the saltiest part of the ocean: the Atlantic. It is the second largest region of the world's ocean. The longest mountain range on Earth is found here: the Mid-Atlantic Ridge.

CHAPTER FOUR

covers the Arctic Ocean, the coldest of all. It is also the smallest and shallowest part of the ocean, and is almost completely surrounded by North America, Europe, and Asia. The creatures here are adapted to life in icy waters.

FACT BOXES give the young reader a quick look at an animal's basic biology: the kind of animal it is, where it lives, how big it is, what it eats, the sounds it makes, and how many young it has at a time.

Colorful **PHOTOGRAPHS** illustrate each spread, supporting the text.

ORANGE CLOWNFISH

This fish and the magnificent sea anemone help each other.

Orange clownfish and magnificent sea anemones live together.

Anemones look like flowers, but they are animals.

Which would you rather pretend to be, a clownfish or an anemone?

36

CLOWNFISH FACTS

KIND OF ANIMAL
fish

HOME
warm, shallow waters in the Pacific and Indian Oceans

SIZE
about as big as the fish in this picture

FOOD
algae, worms, tiny animals

SOUNDS
clicks

EGGS
400 to 1,500 at a time

ANEMONE FACTS

KIND OF ANIMAL
invertebrate

HOME
warm, shallow waters In the Pacific and Indian Oceans

SIZE
about as big around as a saucer sled

FOOD
fish, shrimp, mussels, sea urchins, plankton

SOUNDS
none

EGGS
thousands at a time

PACIFIC OCEAN

Clownfish can **SWIM AROUND**. Sea anemones stay mostly in one place.

37

Interactive **QUESTIONS** in each section encourage conversation about the topic.

POP-UP FACTS sprinkled throughout provide added information about the ocean and the animals featured in each section.

MORE FOR PARENTS

In the back of the book you will find parent tips, with fun activities that relate to ocean topics, a map of the ocean, and a helpful glossary.

CHAPTER 1
PACIFIC OCEAN

The biggest part of Earth's ocean is called the Pacific Ocean. In this chapter you will meet a few of the animals that live there.

FACTS

KIND OF ANIMAL
mammal

HOME
shallow coastal waters
in the northern Pacific

SIZE
weighs about as much
as two four-year-old
children

FOOD
sea urchins, abalone,
mussels, clams, snails,
crabs, squid, octopuses,
fish

SOUNDS
coo, whine, whistle,
growl

BABIES
usually one at a time

When a sea
otter **DIVES,**
its nose and ears
close to keep
water out.

SEA OTTER

A sea otter uses rocks to break open shellfish to eat.

Floating on its back, a sea otter balances a rock on its chest. Then it takes a clam it caught and hits it on the rock. The clamshell breaks open. Time to eat!

The otter gobbles up the clam that lives inside the shell.

Baby sea otters are **BORN** in the water.

To find clams and other shellfish to eat, the sea otter dives down into the ocean. It can hold its breath for a few minutes. Then it pops back up to breathe and eat.

A sea otter grooms its fur to keep it clean. Clean fur helps keep the otter warm.

BABY

GROOMING

KELP is the biggest **SEAWEED** in the ocean. Kelp grows into a seaweed forest in some parts of the ocean.

Sea otters have **WEBBED HIND, OR BACK, FEET.** Webbed feet help otters swim.

Sea otters spend most of their time in the ocean. They sleep floating on the water. Sometimes they gather in large groups. They often use kelp to hold themselves in one spot as the ocean swirls around them.

Have you ever eaten shellfish, such as clams, oysters, scallops, or crabs?

BLUE WHALE

The blue whale is the largest animal that has ever lived.

A blue whale's heart is about the size of **A SMALL CAR.**

A group
of whales is
called
A POD.

This whale is
bigger than the
biggest dinosaur.

A blue whale is
so long that
you could hold
hands with
about 70 friends
to make a ring
around it from
head to tail.

FACTS

KIND OF ANIMAL
mammal

HOME
deep waters in all oceans
except the Arctic

SIZE
about the length of a
medium-size airplane

FOOD
krill

SOUNDS
loudest calls on Earth

BABIES
one at a time

Even though the blue whale is huge, it eats only tiny, shrimplike creatures called krill. A blue whale eats millions of krill in a day.

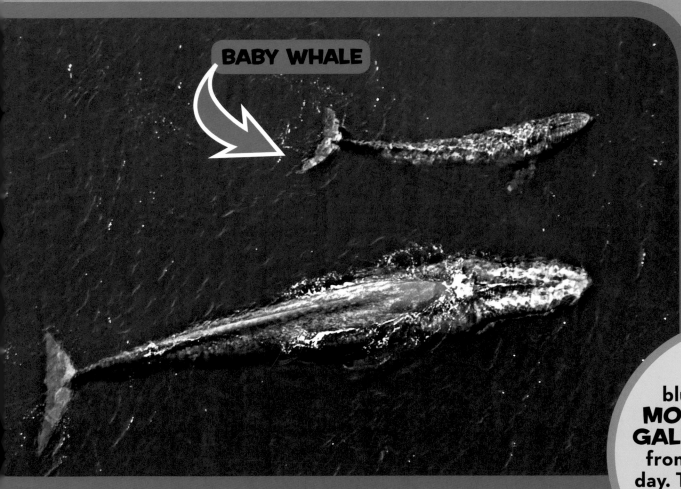

BABY WHALE

MOUTH

A baby blue whale drinks **MORE THAN 100 GALLONS OF MILK** from its mother each day. That is the same as you drinking 1,600 big glasses of milk in a day.

How many glasses of milk, water, or juice do you drink every day?

EYE

The Pacific, Atlantic, Indian, and Arctic Oceans **ARE ALL CONNECTED.** Many kinds of animals (including the blue whale) are found in more than one ocean.

To catch its food, the blue whale swims through huge groups of krill with its mouth wide open. Water and krill flood inside. As the whale closes its mouth, the water flows back out. But the krill stay trapped inside. *Gulp!*

MARINE IGUANA

This iguana is the only lizard that lives in the ocean.

Most marine iguanas are black or dark gray. Some are partly **RED** or **GREEN** or both!

Marine iguanas swim well. Their long tails swoosh from side to side, pushing them through the water.

OCEAN WATER is salty.

The iguanas dive to eat algae that grow on rocks underwater. The iguanas cling to the rocks using their long claws. They scrape the algae off the rocks with their sharp teeth.

EATING UNDERWATER

The lizards cannot **BREATHE** underwater, but they can hold their breath for half an hour.

Marine iguanas get cold swimming in the ocean. They come ashore to warm themselves in the sun.

FACTS

KIND OF ANIMAL
reptile

HOME
shallow coastal waters around the Galápagos Islands, off the coast of South America

SIZE
about as long as a baby's crib

FOOD
seaweed, algae

SOUNDS
none

EGGS
up to six at a time

How do you warm up when you get cold swimming or bathing?

FACTS

KIND OF ANIMAL
mammal

HOME
coastal waters from
Canada to Mexico, and
the Galápagos Islands

SIZE
male: weighs about
as much as five men;
female: smaller

FOOD
fish, squid, octopuses,
shellfish

SOUNDS
bark, grunt, squeal,
belch, growl, bleat,
buzz, click

BABIES
usually one at a time

Ocean waves
are made by the
WIND BLOWING
across the water.
The wind pushes
the water into
moving hills,
or waves.

Sea lions
are **VERY
NOISY**
animals.

20

CALIFORNIA SEA LION

Sea lions are very playful.

Sea lions play in the waves and leap in and out of the water. They are excellent swimmers. California sea lions are faster than any other kind of sea lion or seal.

Sea lions spend most of their time at sea. They hold their breath to dive underwater to catch fish and other food.

Sea lions live in groups. They have their babies on land.

BABY SEA LIONS are almost **BLACK.**

MALE SEA LIONS are **BIGGER AND DARKER** than females.

Have you ever played in the waves at the ocean?

Sometimes hundreds of sea lions gather together on the seashore. When they go back into the ocean, sea lions split up into smaller groups.

DEEPSEA ANGLERFISH

Anglerfish go fishing for food.

Light from the sun does not reach the deep ocean. About a mile down, the ocean is completely dark. The anglerfish is at home here, and has a special way to find food in the dark.

Anglerfish have lots of **SHARP TEETH.**

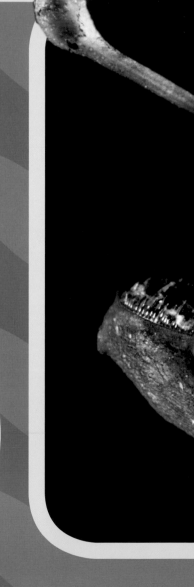

A special, long fin spine called a lure grows from a female anglerfish's head. The end of this lure glows and acts like a fishing rod. The glowing light attracts curious fish right to the anglerfish's mouth.

The male anglerfish depends on the **FEMALE** for food. He does not have a lure.

FACTS

KIND OF ANIMAL
fish

HOME
deep water in much of the ocean

SIZE
female: about the size of the one in the picture at left; male: much smaller

FOOD
fish, squid, other animals

SOUNDS
none known

EGGS
more than a million at a time

Have you ever seen a person using a fishing rod?

FACTS

KIND OF ANIMAL
fish

HOME
shallow coastal waters around southern Australia

SIZE
almost as long as this book is wide

FOOD
sea lice, other tiny creatures

SOUNDS
none known

EGGS
as many as 250 at a time

LEAFY SEA DRAGON

Sea dragons are good at hide-and-seek.

Leafy sea dragons are fish. They look a lot like ocean plants called seaweed that grow where the fish live.

Sea dragons are related to **SEAHORSES.**

Water that moves through the ocean like a river, flowing in one direction, is called a **CURRENT.** The ocean is full of currents.

LEAFY SEA DRAGON

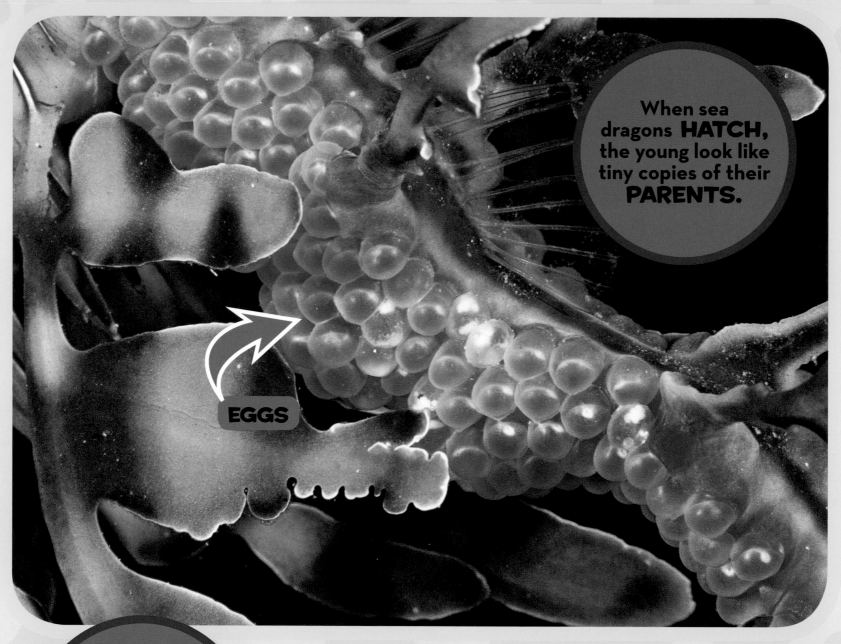

When sea dragons **HATCH,** the young look like tiny copies of their **PARENTS.**

EGGS

The sea dragon looks like the make-believe creature it is named after: **THE DRAGON.**

A sea dragon's body is covered with leaf-shaped parts made of skin. The leafy skin helps the fish blend in with seaweed so that enemies cannot see it.

A sea dragon uses two tiny, see-through fins to swim. One fin is on its back, and the other one is on its neck. The fish is not a strong swimmer. It floats wherever ocean currents take it. It looks like floating seaweed.

Leafy sea dragons have a **NICKNAME: LEAFIES.**

Do you like to play hide-and-seek?

Most kinds of snakes **LAY EGGS.** But a yellow-bellied sea snake's **EGGS STAY INSIDE THE MOTHER,** and the babies are born alive.

There are **NO SEA SNAKES** in the Atlantic Ocean.

The yellow-bellied sea snake is the only kind of sea snake that **LIVES ON BOTH SIDES** of the Pacific Ocean.

Can you move your body like a swimming sea snake?

YELLOW-BELLIED SEA SNAKE

This snake lives in the ocean.

FACTS

KIND OF ANIMAL
reptile

HOME
warm coastal waters
of the Pacific and
Indian Oceans

SIZE
about as long as
four of these open
books lined up

FOOD
fish

SOUNDS
none known

BABIES
as many as ten at a time

Sea snakes swim by moving their long bodies from side to side. They have to come to the surface of the ocean to breathe. But they can also breathe a little bit through their skin underwater.

It is easy to see how this snake got its name. It has a yellow belly.

The yellow-bellied sea snake is a venomous snake, which means its bite is poisonous.

STONY CORAL

Corals are animals that stay attached to one place.

One coral animal is called a polyp (PAH-lip). Each coral polyp is tiny. Its body is soft, like its jellyfish relatives.

POLYP

CORAL REEFS get their color from the colorful algae that grow in them.

A polyp is shaped a bit like a glove. The tentacles of the polyp are like the fingers of a glove. A polyp's hard outer skeleton grows at the end of the tentacles, where the wrist of the glove would be.

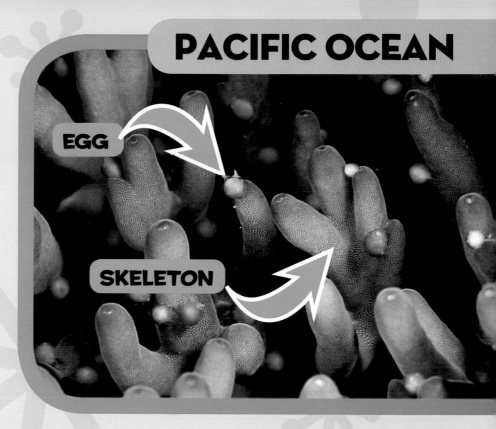

EGG

SKELETON

FACTS

KIND OF ANIMAL
invertebrate

HOME
mostly in warm, shallow waters of the Atlantic, Pacific, and Indian Oceans

SIZE
range from as tiny as the word SIZE above to as long as a man's foot

FOOD
tiny plants and animals

SOUNDS
none known

BABIES
millions of eggs at a time

A coral polyp attaches to a rock or to an old coral skeleton. After hundreds of years, corals can grow into huge, underwater neighborhoods called coral reefs.

Can you draw a colorful coral reef?

There are more than 2,000 kinds of **STONY CORAL.** Many different kinds live near each other in a reef. Here are a few kinds of stony coral found in **EARTH'S OCEAN.**

CUP

PLATE

CABBAGE

DISK

ELKHORN

MADREPORA

ORANGE CLOWNFISH

This fish and the magnificent sea anemone help each other.

Orange clownfish and magnificent sea anemones live together.

Anemones look like flowers, but they are animals.

Which would you rather pretend to be, a clownfish or an anemone?

CLOWNFISH FACTS

KIND OF ANIMAL
fish

HOME
warm, shallow waters in the Pacific and Indian Oceans

SIZE
about as big as the fish in this picture

FOOD
algae, worms, tiny animals

SOUNDS
clicks

EGGS
400 to 1,500 at a time

ANEMONE FACTS

KIND OF ANIMAL
invertebrate

HOME
warm, shallow waters in the Pacific and Indian Oceans

SIZE
about as big around as a saucer sled

FOOD
fish, shrimp, mussels, sea urchins, plankton

SOUNDS
none

EGGS
thousands at a time

Clownfish can **SWIM AROUND**. Sea anemones stay mostly in one place.

A sea anemone has tentacles that sting most kinds of animals that come close to it. But it does not sting the clownfish. The anemone protects its clownfish from other fish that might want to eat it.

ANOTHER NAME for clownfish is ANEMONEFISH.

The orange clownfish may trick other kinds of fish to come close to the anemone. The anemone eats those fish.

Clownfish and anemones usually live in **CORAL REEFS.**

The anemone helps protect the clownfish, and the clownfish helps feed the anemone. This kind of relationship is called symbiosis (sim–bee–OH–sis).

39

FACTS

KIND OF ANIMAL
mammal

HOME
mainly in cold waters, both coastal and open sea, throughout Earth's ocean

SIZE
almost as long as a school bus

FOOD
fish, seals, sea lions, walruses, seabirds, other whales

SOUNDS
squeal, trill, whistle, scream, roar, squawk, and other noises

BABIES
one at a time

ORCA

This animal is the largest kind of dolphin.

Orcas are also called killer whales. They are hunters that work together to catch their food.

If orcas spot a seal resting on a floating piece of ice, they speed toward it together. They make a wave to wash the seal off the ice and into the ocean where they can catch it.

Orcas live where the ocean is **VERY COLD.**

A baby orca is born underwater. The baby knows how to swim as soon as it is born. But its mother helps guide it to the surface to take its first breath.

Orcas are marine mammals. Like all mammals, they must breathe air. They live their whole lives in the ocean. But they come to the surface of the ocean to breathe.

Orcas have a thick layer of **FAT, CALLED BLUBBER.** The blubber helps keep an orca warm.

An orca **TOOTH** can be as long as **FOUR INCHES.**

Have you ever held your breath to go underwater while you were swimming?

WANDERING ALBATROSS

This seabird spends almost its whole life flying over the ocean.

A wandering albatross has **SUPERLONG WINGS—** the longest of any bird.

Its long wings help the wandering albatross soar over the ocean for hours at a time. The bird hardly has to flap its wings. It glides using the wind to stay in the air.

FACTS

KIND OF ANIMAL
bird

HOME
southern part of the
ocean near Antarctica

SIZE
wing tip to wing tip,
stretches longer than
a king-size bed

FOOD
octopuses, squid, fish

SOUNDS
scream, whistle, grunt,
bill-clap

CHICKS
one at a time

Wandering albatross parents stay together as if they were married. After the mother lays an egg, both parents take turns keeping it warm. When the egg hatches, the parents take turns flying off to find food. One stays at the nest to guard the chick.

The wandering albatross **FLOATS** on the ocean surface when it eats. It nests on land to raise its **CHICKS.**

What kinds of things do you take turns doing?

CHAPTER 2
ATLANTIC OCEAN

The second biggest part of the ocean is the Atlantic. It is also the saltiest.
Let's take a look at a few animals you might see there.

CARIBBEAN REEF
OCTOPUS

This animal changes color to match its surroundings.

A fish might swim right by a Caribbean reef octopus without seeing it. That's because the octopus can change its color and pattern to match the things around it.

EYE

To catch animals to eat, the reef octopus makes an **UMBRELLA-SHAPED** net with its arms.

FACTS

KIND OF ANIMAL
invertebrate

HOME
warm, shallow waters in the western Atlantic and parts of the Pacific

SIZE
weighs about as much as 12 sticks of butter

FOOD
crabs, shrimp, lobsters, fish

SOUNDS
none

EGGS
100 to 500 at a time

The octopus blends in so well that it's almost invisible. The predator, or animal that hunts and eats other animals, doesn't see it. The reef octopus is safe.

Can you count how many arms this octopus has?

MANATEE MOTHERS push their newborns up to the surface to take their first breath.

WEST INDIAN MANATEE

This marine mammal lives in rivers and the ocean.

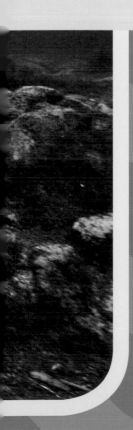

Water in the ocean is salty. Water in rivers usually is not. Most water animals live in one or the other. But the West Indian manatee can live in both.

FACTS:

KIND OF ANIMAL
mammal

HOME
warm coastal waters along the southeastern United States; sometimes in rivers

SIZE
weighs about as much as seven women

FOOD
mostly plants, some fish and other small animals

SOUNDS
squeak, squeal, grunt

BABIES
usually one at a time, sometimes two

This mammal has a big, round body and a flat tail. A manatee flaps its tail up and down to swim. It steers with two flippers on the sides of its body.

A manatee eats about **100 POUNDS** of food a day. That's like you eating **400 HAMBURGERS** in a day!

Manatees can hold their breath for about **FIVE MINUTES** at a time to eat plants growing underwater.

A MANATEE BABY stays with its mother for about two years.

Manatee babies are born underwater. When a newborn manatee is born, it weighs about 65 pounds. That is as much as eight newborn human babies.

Can you name some plants that you eat? (HINT: Vegetables and fruits are plants.)

There are more than **360 SPECIES,** or kinds, of sharks in the ocean.

GREAT WHITE SHARK

Great whites are the biggest meat-eating fish.

FACTS

KIND OF ANIMAL
fish

HOME
mostly in cool, coastal waters throughout the world, also in open ocean

SIZE
about as long as a minivan

FOOD
fish, seals, penguins, sea lions, dolphins, porpoises

SOUNDS
none

BABIES
2 to 10 at a time

Fierce-looking great white sharks might look scary, but they do not like to eat people. They do like to eat fish, seals, and even penguins.

FIN

This shark gets its name from its big size and its white belly. A great white shark has a dark back and a light belly. Its color helps it sneak up on prey.

Great white sharks have about **300 TEETH** that grow in several rows.

If a fish or other prey looks up, the shark's white belly blends in with the light from the surface of the ocean. If a fish looks down, the shark's dark back blends in with the darker waters below it.

Great white sharks often **LEAP** out of the water as they grab their prey.

Life in the ocean is all connected. For example, tiny plants called phytoplankton turn sunlight into food. Small fish eat phytoplankton. Seals eat those small fish. Then great white sharks eat the seals. This is called a food web.

Can you think of a food web on land? (HINT: What does a zebra eat? What eats zebras?)

ATLANTIC PUFFIN

This little bird swims underwater and flies through the air.

Puffins are nicknamed **"CLOWNS** of the ocean" and **"SEA PARROTS."**

Puffins live on the ocean, far away from land, all winter long. They have webbed feet, like ducks. They can swim underwater, float on the surface, and fly.

A puffin can carry back as many as **30 FISH** at a time to feed its chick.

FACTS

KIND OF ANIMAL
bird

HOME
North Atlantic. Winter: deep, icy water far from land; Summer: rocky cliffs on the coast

SIZE
about as long as a Chihuahua, a little dog

FOOD
mainly fish

SOUNDS
purr, grunt, groan

CHICKS
usually one at a time

The birds dive underwater and swim to chase the fish they eat.

ATLANTIC OCEAN

SWIMMING PUFFIN

During the spring and summer, puffins make underground nests called burrows. They lay eggs and raise chicks in these burrows. Parents take turns catching fish to feed their chicks.

PUFFIN CHICK

When a **PUFFIN CHICK** is about 50 days old, it is on its own.

Why do you think puffins have the nicknames they do?

ATLANTIC SPOTTED DOLPHIN

Spotted dolphins live in groups called pods.

Some adult spotted dolphins have so many spots, they almost look all **WHITE.**

Sometimes a hundred spotted dolphins travel together in a group. These groups are called pods. More often the pods are smaller. Spotted dolphins usually have at least a few other dolphins around.

Dolphins are very playful. They leap out of the water and fall back in with a splash. They even follow boats to play alongside.

FACTS

KIND OF ANIMAL
mammal

HOME
mostly in warm, shallow waters of the Atlantic; also found in deep water

SIZE
about as long as three tricycles in a row

FOOD
fish, squid, other small animals

SOUNDS
whistle, click, chirp, whine, squeal

BABIES
one at a time

Baby **SPOTTED DOLPHINS** do not have spots.

Do you remember what the largest kind of dolphin is? (HINT: see page 41.)

There are more than 30 different species of dolphins. Here are just a few.

WHITE-SIDED

BOTTLENOSE

DUSKY

SHORT-BEAKED

ROUGH-TOOTHED

SPINNER

ATLANTIC HORSESHOE CRAB

Horseshoe crabs are related to spiders.

FACTS

KIND OF ANIMAL
invertebrate

HOME
coastal waters of eastern North America

SIZE
weighs a little more than two of these books

FOOD
mollusks, worms, fish, and other small animals

SOUNDS
none

EGGS
thousands at a time

This odd-looking creature has a shell shaped like a horseshoe, a long tail, and five pairs of "legs." (A pair means two.)

The horseshoe crab's first four pairs of legs have claws and help the animal walk.

LEGS

Horseshoe crabs are most **ACTIVE** at night.

SAND DOLLARS

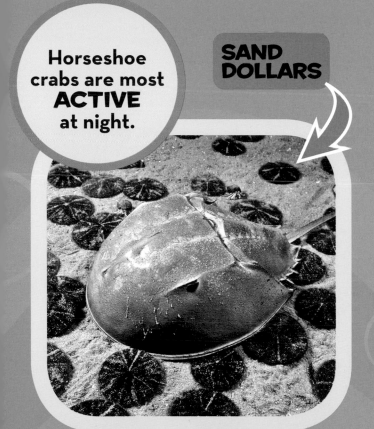

The last pair has paddle-shaped ends. The horseshoe crab uses those to push itself along on the bottom of the ocean, where it looks for food.

In the spring, horseshoe crabs come ashore in big groups to **LAY EGGS** in the sand on beaches.

How many legs does the horseshoe crab have?

ANTARCTIC KRILL

Tiny krill are food for many larger marine animals.

Krill means **"WHALE FOOD"** in the language spoken in the country of Norway.

Krill are small, but they are very important in the ocean food web.

Billions (that is a lot!) of krill swim together in huge groups. Animals as big as blue whales eat them.

Krill eat tiny plants and animals, called phytoplankton and zooplankton, that make their own food from sunlight.

UNDER ICE

Krill can **SWIM** for weeks without stopping.

FACTS

KIND OF ANIMAL
invertebrate

HOME
ocean all around Antarctica

SIZE
about the length of the word KRILL in the title on page 66

FOOD
phytoplankton, zooplankton

SOUNDS
none known

EGGS
thousands at a time

What is the tiniest kind of food that you eat?

CHINSTRAP PENGUIN

Penguins are birds, but they cannot fly.

Most of a chinstrap's **DIVES** last for about 30 seconds.

Penguins are expert swimmers. They use their wings to swim in the ocean. They dive to catch fish and other food.

Chinstraps live in the very cold ocean around Antarctica.

A chinstrap penguin's feathers fit tightly together all over its body. They keep the penguin warm. The bird has a layer of fat under its skin that also helps keep it warm.

FACTS

KIND OF ANIMAL
bird

HOME
both deep and coastal waters around Antarctica

SIZE
about as tall as a one-year-old child

FOOD
mostly krill; also squid, fish, shrimp

SOUNDS
cackle, hum, hiss

CHICKS
usually two at a time

Can you point to the part of this penguin that gave the chinstrap its name?

There are 17 species of penguins. Here are a few others that live in the southern ocean around Antarctica.

Many penguins live in the ocean at the bottom of the world. Sometimes it is called the **SOUTHERN OCEAN.** But most ocean scientists call it part of the Pacific and Atlantic Oceans.

EMPEROR

MACARONI

ADÉLIE

KING

GENTOO

GRAY SEAL

Baby gray seals are born white.

FACTS

KIND OF ANIMAL
mammal

HOME
cold coastal waters in
the North Atlantic

SIZE
male: weighs about
as much as three
professional football
players; female:
smaller

FOOD
fish, crustaceans,
squid, octopuses

SOUNDS
hoot

BABIES
one at a time

Baby seals are called pups. A pup's fur is soft and thick. It keeps the pup warm on the ice or land where it was born, but it would not keep it warm in the water.

A **BABY SEAL** can gain 100 pounds in three weeks.

By the time a pup is a month old, it grows new fur that is gray and waterproof.

Now it can swim. A thick layer of fat under its skin—blubber—helps keep a gray seal warm in the icy cold water where it lives.

Adult male, or boy, gray seals are usually darker than females, or girls. Many adults have spots.

Gray seals can hold their **BREATH** for 20 minutes.

There are three main groups of **GRAY SEALS** in different parts of the Atlantic Ocean.

When you were born, was your hair the same color it is now?

A sponge has three layers. The middle layer is **JELLYLIKE** and gives the sponge its shape.

FACTS

KIND OF ANIMAL
invertebrate

HOME
shallow waters in the Caribbean Sea and Gulf of Mexico

SIZE
grows about as tall as a two-and-a-half-year-old child

FOOD
plankton

SOUNDS
none

EGGS
thousands at a time

An animal that lives in **ONE SPOT** and does not move around is called a sessile animal.

YELLOW TUBE SPONGE

A sponge is an animal.

A yellow tube sponge attaches itself to the ocean floor, where it lives its whole life.

It is a very simple animal. A sponge's body does not have very many parts. Sponges do not have hearts, stomachs, or brains like people do.

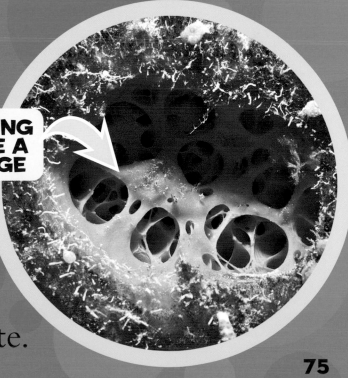

LOOKING INSIDE A SPONGE

Water flows through a sponge. The water brings in food and carries out waste.

There are about 5,000 species of sponges. They come in many shapes, colors, and sizes. Here are just a few.

ELEPHANT EAR

HEDGEHOG

PINK VASE

BARREL

STAGHORN

AZURE VASE

Different kinds of sponges have **DIFFERENT SHAPES,** including fans, tubes, cups, and cones.

Can you think of another sessile animal in this book? (HINT: See page 32.)

CHAPTER 3
INDIAN OCEAN

The Indian Ocean is the third largest ocean. It formed
about 65 million years ago, making it the youngest ocean.

FACTS

KIND OF ANIMAL
fish

HOME
warm, shallow waters
throughout the ocean

SIZE
wing tip to wing tip,
stretches longer than
three king-size beds

FOOD
mainly plankton

SOUNDS
none known

BABIES
one, sometimes two,
at a time

REMORAS are a kind of fish that **HANG ON TO RAYS,** traveling with them. They eat whatever falls out of the ray's mouth. **FREE DINNER!**

GIANT OCEANIC MANTA RAY

The ray is a fish that "flies" through the ocean.

The giant oceanic manta ray is the largest kind of ray. Its fins look like wings as the fish swims through the water, flapping them up and down.

FLAPS

When it wants to eat, the manta ray unrolls special flaps on each side of its mouth. The flaps help aim water into its mouth.

81

As water leaves a manta ray's mouth, it passes through gill rakers, or strainers. The gill rakers trap plankton inside the ray's mouth as the water flows back out.

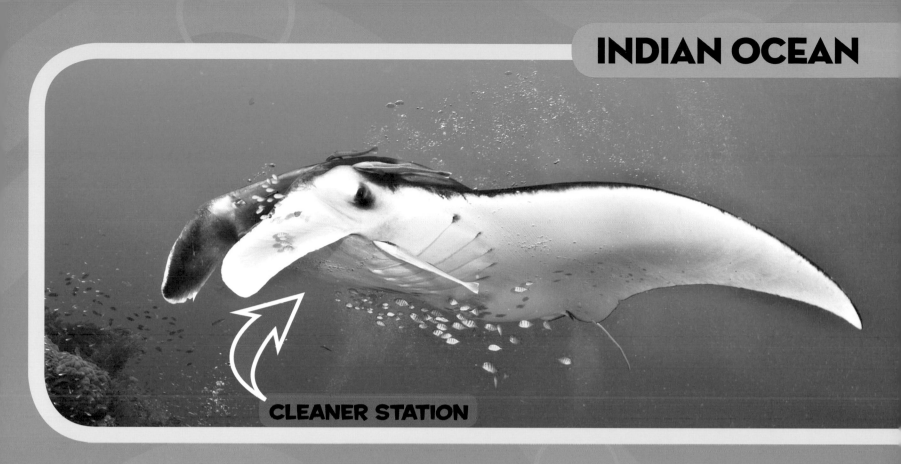

CLEANER STATION

MANTA RAYS can jump as high as seven feet out of the water.

Manta rays often visit "cleaner stations," where small, hungry fish hang out. These fish clean the rays by nibbling off tiny animals called parasites stuck to the ray's body.

How is a car wash like a fish cleaner station?

FACTS

KIND OF ANIMAL
fish

HOME
near the ocean floor in warm, shallow waters in the Atlantic, Pacific, and Indian Oceans

SIZE
almost as long as this book is wide

FOOD
mollusks, sea urchins, crabs, snails, hermit crabs

SOUNDS
none known

EGGS
hundreds at a time

CALM

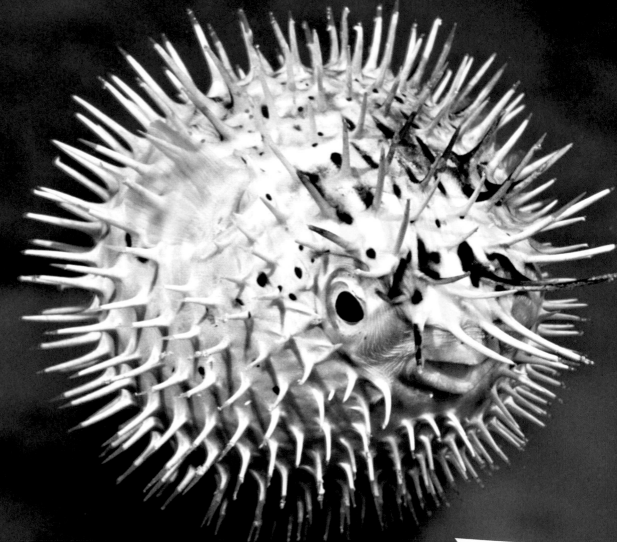

BALLOON-FISH is another name for porcupinefish.

How can you make yourself look bigger than you are?

DEFENDING ITSELF

LONG-SPINE PORCUPINEFISH

When it swallows water, this fish blows up like a balloon.

A porcupinefish has two different looks. It looks like one kind of fish when it is swimming around calmly.

When an enemy comes near, the porcupinefish takes in a big gulp of water.

Suddenly, the skinny fish becomes big, round, and covered with sharp spines. Most predators do not want to bite a big, prickly fish.

The fish has a **BEAK** that helps it break open the shells of the **FOOD** it eats.

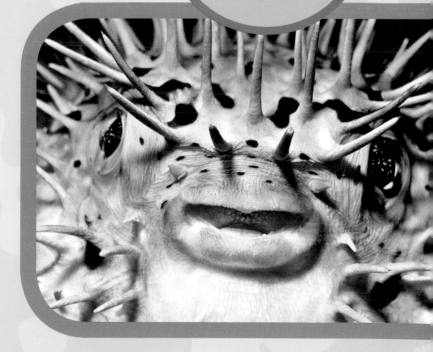

WHALE SHARK

Whale sharks have **27,000 LITTLE TEETH** in 300 rows.

This is the largest fish.

FACTS

KIND OF ANIMAL
fish

HOME
warm ocean waters,
mostly near the Equator

SIZE
about as long as a big
school bus

FOOD
mainly plankton

SOUNDS
none

BABIES
up to 300 at a time

The whale shark is not a whale. It is a shark, which means the whale shark is a fish. It got its name because it is as big as some kinds of whales.

87

This huge shark is not a dangerous animal. It is a filter-feeder. It filters, or separates, its food from water like a strainer. It eats plankton—the small plants and animals that float wherever ocean currents take them.

How wide can you open your mouth?

PHYTO-PLANKTON are tiny plants. **ZOOPLANKTON** are tiny animals. **PLANKTON** includes both.

Whale sharks have very wide mouths. The fish opens its huge mouth to let the ocean water in. It filters plankton from the water as water flows back out through its gills.

Most kinds of sea stars have **FIVE ARMS,** but others have up to forty!

FACTS

KIND OF ANIMAL
invertebrate

HOME
coral reefs and sea grass beds in shallow waters

SIZE
about the size of a small bike tire

FOOD
plankton

SOUNDS
none

EGGS
thousands at a time

BLUE STAR

This sea star hides during the day and moves at night.

Sea stars are often called starfish. But they are not fish. They are echinoderms (eh-KIE-noh-derms), a group of marine animals that includes sand dollars, sea cucumbers, and sea urchins.

If an enemy bites off one of a blue star's five arms, the sea star can grow a new one. This amazing ability is called regeneration.

A sea star's mouth is on the **UNDERSIDE** of its body, in the middle of its five arms.

There are more than a **THOUSAND** kinds of **SEA STARS.** They come in many shapes, colors, and sizes. Here are just a few.

CHOCOLATE CHIP

BAT STARS

RED

SLENDER GREEN

COMET

SUN

Which of these sea stars is your favorite?

COMMON LIONFISH

This fish has spines with poison in them.

The common lionfish is also called the **DEVIL FIREFISH.**

This pretty fish's pokey spines help protect it from predators— enemies that might want to eat it.

Can you find the lionfish's eye in this picture?

Lionfish are predators, too. They generally hunt for food at night. They use their long fins to trap their food.

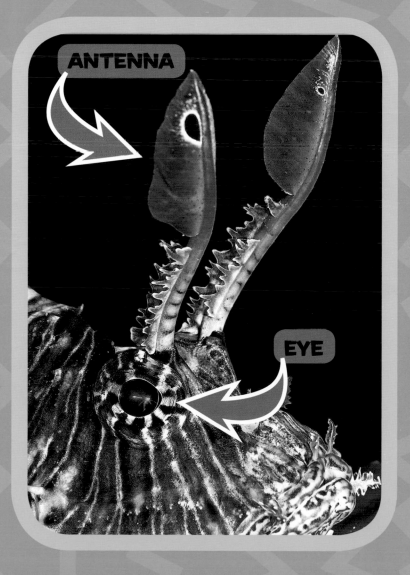

ANTENNA

EYE

The common lionfish is now **FOUND** in the Atlantic Ocean because people brought it there.

FACTS

KIND OF ANIMAL
fish

HOME
shallow muddy waters in the Indian Ocean and South Pacific, and in parts of the Atlantic

SIZE
about as long as a loaf of bread

FOOD
small fish and other animals

SOUNDS
none

EGGS
about 15,000 at a time

What do you remember reading about sponges?
(HINT: See page 74.)

HAWKSBILL SEA TURTLE

This turtle's mouth looks like a hawk's bill.

Hawksbill sea turtles use their pointed bills, or beaks, to reach into narrow places to get food. They especially like to eat sponges.

97

MOTHER MAKES A NEST

BABY HAWKSBILL SEA TURTLES cannot dive deep. They FLOAT near the ocean's surface.

EGGS IN NEST

Sea turtles spend their whole lives at sea. The only time female sea turtles come ashore is when they dig a nest for their eggs on a beach. Male sea turtles never come ashore.

The other kinds of sea turtles are the Kemp's ridley, olive ridley, **GREEN,** leatherback, **LOGGERHEAD,** and flatback.

FACTS

KIND OF ANIMAL
reptile

HOME
in and near coral reefs and along coastlines in warm parts of the Indian, Atlantic, and Pacific Oceans

SIZE
weigh about as much as a man

FOOD
mostly sponges; also fish, jellyfish, and other small sea animals

SOUNDS
none

EGGS
about 140 in one nest

There are seven kinds of sea turtles. Many people think the hawksbill's shell is the most beautiful of the seven.

CHAPTER 4
ARCTIC OCEAN

The Arctic Ocean is the smallest and coldest ocean.

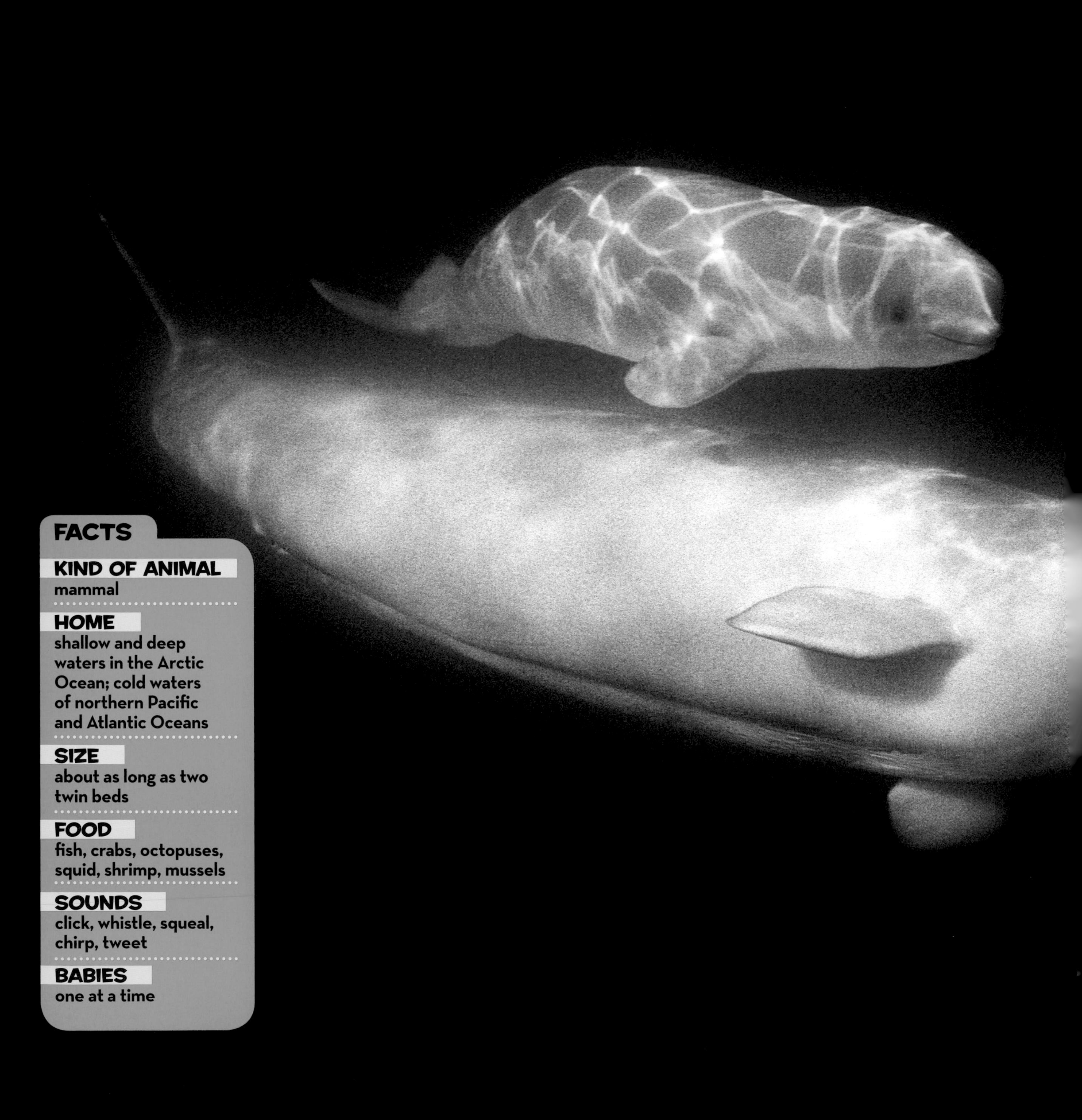

FACTS

KIND OF ANIMAL
mammal

HOME
shallow and deep
waters in the Arctic
Ocean; cold waters
of northern Pacific
and Atlantic Oceans

SIZE
about as long as two
twin beds

FOOD
fish, crabs, octopuses,
squid, shrimp, mussels

SOUNDS
click, whistle, squeal,
chirp, tweet

BABIES
one at a time

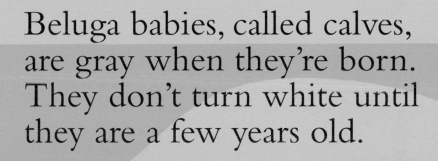

BELUGA

Belugas are small, white whales.

Beluga babies, called calves, are gray when they're born. They don't turn white until they are a few years old.

During the coldest part of the year, much of the Arctic Ocean is covered by ice. Big groups of belugas swim south until they find open water.

A thick layer of blubber helps keep belugas warm in the **ICY COLD** water where they live.

BABY BELUGA

The beluga is sometimes called the **SEA CANARY,** because it makes tweeting sounds like the bird called a **CANARY.**

Because belugas are mammals, they have to be able to breathe at the surface. So they cannot stay where the ocean surface is completely frozen.

The beluga's **BIG, ROUND** forehead's fat is called a melon.

Can you name three things that are white?

WALRUS

Walruses have two very long teeth called tusks.

Walrus tusks can grow to be three feet long—about as long as two copies of this book opened side by side. Both male and female walruses have tusks.

FACTS

KIND OF ANIMAL
mammal

HOME
Arctic Ocean and northern Atlantic and Pacific Oceans

SIZE
male: weighs as much as a small car; female: smaller

FOOD
clams, mussels, shrimp, crabs, tubeworms, soft corals, and other animals

SOUNDS
whistle, growl, click, grunt, tap, bark

BABIES
usually one at a time

Walruses spend most of their lives in the ocean. When they do leave the water, they can use their tusks to help pull their big bodies out.

A walrus baby, called a **CALF**, weighs more than **100 POUNDS** when it is born.

WHISKERS

Walruses use their whiskers to feel for food on the ocean floor.

How much did you weigh when you were born?

NARWHAL

A narwhal has only two teeth.

FACTS

KIND OF ANIMAL
mammal

HOME
in water under ice in
the winter; close to
shore in the summer

SIZE
male: weighs about as
much as a small car;
female: smaller

FOOD
fish, shrimp, squid

SOUNDS
click, whistle, squeak

BABIES
one at a time

Narwhals
are close
relatives of
BELUGAS.

To eat, a narwhal sucks food, such as fish, into its
mouth. Since it has only two teeth, it does not chew.

One of the male narwhal's two teeth grows very long. It is called a tusk. It looks like a unicorn's horn.

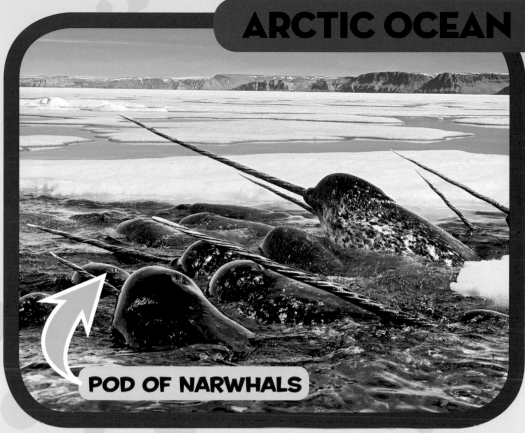

POD OF NARWHALS

POLAR BEARS and orcas hunt narwhals.

NARWHALS AT A BREATHING HOLE

The female narwhal may grow a tusk, but it is not very long.

Is a unicorn a real animal or a make-believe animal?

A **NARWHAL'S TUSK** can be nine feet long—about as long as three baseball bats.

Two male narwhals often rub their tusks together as if they were sword-fighting. Scientists think this may help narwhals know which is the strongest male in a group.

Narwhals make some of the **DEEPEST DIVES** of all marine mammals.

ARCTIC COD

This fish lives farther north than any other kind of fish.

Do you like to eat fish?

Belugas and **NARWHALS EAT** arctic cod.

Arctic cod live under the ice of the Arctic Ocean. These fish survive best in very cold water. They have been found near the North Pole.

FACTS

KIND OF ANIMAL
fish

HOME
usually near the surface

SIZE
about as long as this page is wide

FOOD
plankton, krill

SOUNDS
males grunt

EGGS
as many as 21,000 at a time

Arctic cod sometimes **SWIM TOGETHER** in large groups called schools.

Arctic cod hide in cracks that form **UNDERWATER** in the **SEA ICE** that covers the surface of the Arctic Ocean.

One of the most important things about these fish is that they are food for many other animals that live in the Arctic Ocean.

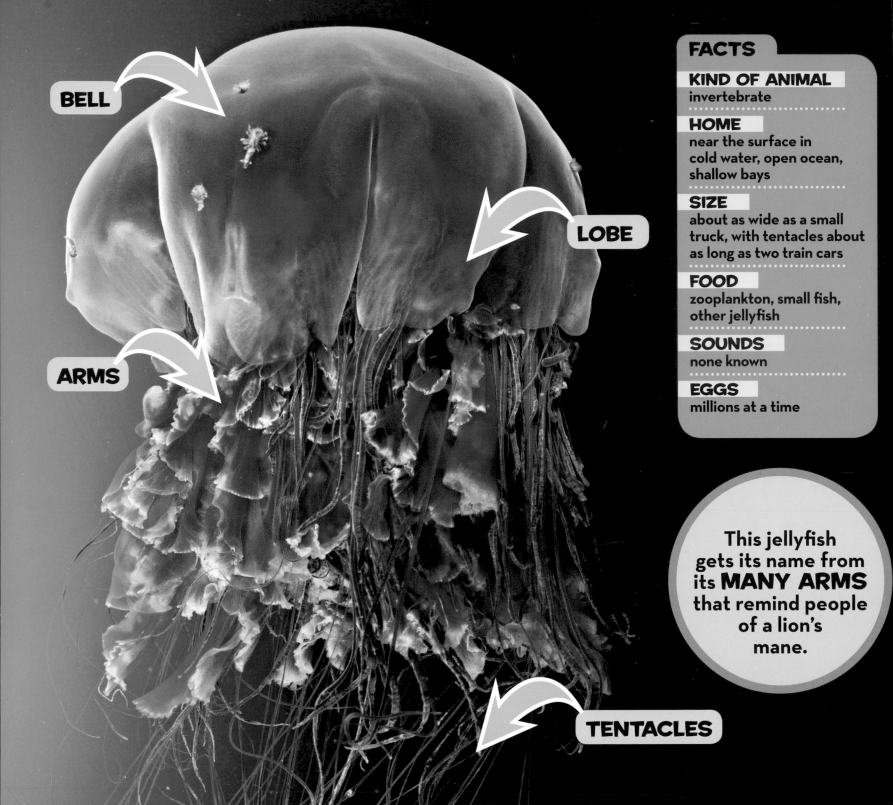

BELL

LOBE

ARMS

TENTACLES

This jellyfish
gets its name from
its **MANY ARMS**
that remind people
of a lion's
mane.

How do you put food into your mouth?

LION'S MANE JELLYFISH

This is one of the largest kinds of jellyfish.

A jellyfish's body is called the bell. The lion's mane jellyfish's bell is divided into eight parts. Each part, called a lobe, has about 100 tentacles.

To eat, a jellyfish captures its prey with its long tentacles. It has shorter ones called arms that take the food from the tentacles and put it into the jellyfish's mouth.

A lion's mane jellyfish lives for only **ONE YEAR.**

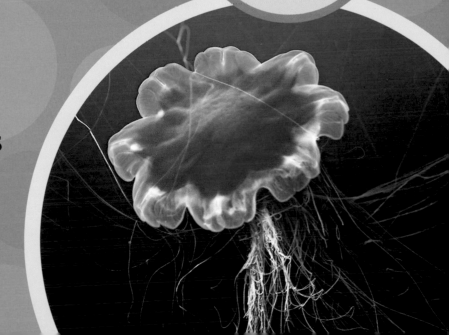

There are more than 400 kinds of jellyfish. Here are just a few of them.

CROWN

LAGOON

PURPLE-STRIPED

SEA NETTLE

UPSIDE-DOWN

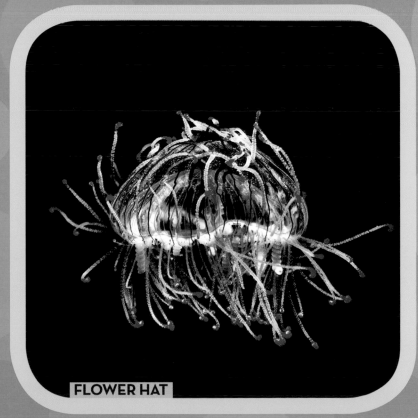
FLOWER HAT

10 COOL THINGS TO REMEMBER ABOUT THE OCEAN!

1 Almost all the **WATER** on Earth is in the ocean.

2 Earth looks like a **BLUE MARBLE** from space because the ocean covers most of it.

3 Most of the **OXYGEN,** or the air we breathe, was made by plants in the ocean.

4 **SAND** is made up of tiny bits of rocks, minerals, plants, and animals.

5 Everything that lives on Earth, including you, depends on **THE OCEAN.**

6 High **MOUNTAINS,** deep valleys, canyons, ridges, and huge, flat plains make up the **FLOOR** of the ocean.

7
Water **EVAPORATES**— it leaves the ocean and mixes with the air. It does that when water becomes **VAPOR**— kind of like the steam you see when water boils. Then water **FALLS BACK** to Earth as rain, sleet, hail, and snow.

8
There are different parts of the ocean, but they are **ALL CONNECTED.** The main parts of the ocean are called the Pacific, Atlantic, Indian, and Arctic.

9
Most of the **LIVING THINGS** on Earth live in the ocean. They range in size from being too small to see without a microscope to the largest animal known— **THE BLUE WHALE.**

10
Only a tiny part of the ocean has been **EXPLORED.** There are huge parts of the big ocean that no human has ever seen.

PARENT TIPS

Extend your child's experience beyond the pages of this book. A visit to the beach is one great way to continue satisfying your child's curiosity about the ocean and its wildlife. Take walks along the beach and encourage conversation—using all five senses—about the ocean's crashing waves, salty sea spray, pretty seashells, the feel of sand under bare feet, and the fresh smell of sea air. Explore interesting tidal pools, watch crabs digging into the sand, and try to identify shorebirds. Here are some other activities you can do with the *National Geographic Kids First Big Book of the Ocean*.

HIDE-AND-SEEK
(SEARCH STRATEGY)

Sea dragons and octopuses are two of several animals in the book that "play hide-and-seek." The game is a fun one for children to play, and there are variations you can use to accommodate your child's age and your surroundings. Play the traditional way if your surroundings are appropriate, or hide a small object and give clues to your child as she looks for it. You can play hide-and-seek in plain sight, using camouflage by placing objects on or among things that are the same color (e.g., a white button you hide on a crumpled white tissue). Take turns with your child hiding and seeking.

SWIM LIKE AN ANIMAL
(EXERCISE)

Most of the animals in this book swim. As you and your child play in a pool, the ocean, or even a bathtub, help him demonstrate how different animals swim. He can pretend to be a penguin, using his arms as wings to "fly" through the water. Help him float to be a leafy sea dragon, letting currents move him through the ocean. As a marine iguana, he can hold his legs together and swish them from side to side like the lizard uses its tail to propel it through the sea.

CREATE A REEF
(ARTS AND CRAFTS)

Make a colorful reef collage with your child. Visit a craft store together to find a variety of brightly colored items to create her piece of art. With a glue stick handy, use poster board as the base, construction paper to create colorful fish, and items such as feathers, beads, and sequins for coral. Let your child help pick the items as you shop, and let her be the art director as you work on the collage. Ask for her input and advice often as you help her create her work of art.

FIND "YOUR" OCEAN
(GEOGRAPHY)

Look at a map with your child to illustrate where the ocean is in relation to where you live. Show him his hometown and point to the route you'd use to get to the sea. Show him any rivers in the area that flow to the sea. Discuss which ocean you live closest to, and remind him what animals are in the corresponding chapter in this book.

MEASURE A BLUE WHALE
(MATH)

A blue whale can grow to be 100 feet long. Help your child visualize how big that is by measuring 100 feet outside. Have her help you measure. Mark the distance. Time how long it takes your child to run the whale's length. Count together how many steps your child takes as she walks the length of the whale. Compare the length of the blue whale to the largest fish: The whale shark grows to about 40 feet long.

GO FISH
(HAND-EYE COORDINATION)

Anglerfish use a lure to attract prey. Pretend to be an anglerfish. Play this game with a flashlight in the dark. Have your child (the anglerfish) sit cross-legged on the floor. Place a flashlight on the floor across from him. From the dark, roll a small ball or large marble (prey) across the beam of light, close to your child. He tries to grab it without moving from his seated position, and only while the ball is in the light. Do it a few times, then switch roles. Who catches the most prey?

PLAY CONCENTRATION
(MEMORY)

There are seven species of sea turtles. Make a deck of sea turtle cards with your child. Use large index cards so there is room to draw on them. Help your child make two cards for each of the seven turtle species. Leaving one side of each card blank, have her draw turtles on the other side. Help her write all their names: hawksbill, loggerhead, leatherback, Kemp's ridley, green, olive ridley, and flatback. Then play the card game "Concentration."

MANTA RAYS

SING BABY BELUGA
(MUSIC)

If you and your child already know the song "Baby Beluga," by Raffi Cavoukian, sing it together. If you don't, learn it together. The tune is available online. Other fun songs to sing about the ocean that are easy to find online include "Down by the Bay," "Hole in the Middle of the Sea," and "Slippery Fish."

VISIT ONLINE
(TECHNOLOGY)

Explore more about the ocean with your child here:

kids.nationalgeographic.com/kids/activities/new/ocean/

oceanservice.noaa.gov/education/welcome.html
neok12.com/Oceans.htm

OCEAN MAP

Using this map, you can find the parts of the ocean where the animals in this book often live.

NORTH AMERICA

ATLANTIC OCEAN

PACIFIC OCEAN

SOUTH AMERICA

A R C

ATLANT
OCEAN

PACIFIC

sea otter
blue whale
marine iguana
California sea lion
deepsea anglerfish
leafy sea dragon
yellow-bellied sea snake
stony coral
orange clownfish
magnificent sea anemone
orca
wandering albatross
Caribbean reef octopus
great white shark
Antarctic krill
chinstrap penguin
giant oceanic manta ray
long-spine porcupinefish
whale shark
blue star
common lionfish
hawksbill sea turtle
walrus

ATLANTIC

blue whale
deepsea anglerfish
stony coral
orca
wandering albatross
Caribbean reef octopus

West Indian manatee
great white shark
Atlantic puffin
Atlantic spotted dolphin
Atlantic horseshoe crab
Antarctic krill
chinstrap penguin

EAN

EUROPE

ASIA

AFRICA

PACIFIC
OCEAN

INDIAN
OCEAN

AUSTRALIA

ARCTIC
orca
beluga
walrus
narwhal
arctic cod
lion's mane jellyfish

INDIAN
blue whale
deepsea anglerfish
yellow-bellied sea snake
stony coral
orange clownfish
magnificent sea anemone
orca
great white shark
giant oceanic manta ray
long-spine porcupinefish
whale shark
blue star
common lionfish
hawksbill sea turtle

gray seal
yellow tube sponge
long-spine porcupinefish
whale shark
hawksbill sea turtle
walrus
lion's mane jellyfish

GLOSSARY

ALGAE
a group of organisms that usually grow in water, such as kelp and other seaweed

BIRDS
a group of warm-blooded, vertebrate animals that have feathers, wings, and lay eggs; most can fly

BLUBBER
the fat on large sea animals, such as whales

COASTAL
close to where land meets the ocean

CRUSTACEANS
a large group of animals, such as lobsters and crabs, with a hard outer skeleton, pairs of legs or claws on each segment of the body, and two pairs of antennae

CURRENT
water that moves through the ocean like a river, flowing in one direction

FISH
cold-blooded, vertebrate animals that live in water and breathe through gills

INVERTEBRATES
animals without spinal columns, or backbones

KELP
kinds of large seaweed

MAMMALS
a group of vertebrate animals, including humans, that are warm-blooded, breathe air, have hair, and nurse their young

MOLLUSKS
a group of invertebrate animals; usually have a soft body protected by a shell; includes snails and clams

OCEAN
the salt water that covers almost three-quarters of the Earth's surface

PHYTOPLANKTON
plankton made up of plants

PLANKTON
tiny plants and animals that live in water

POD
group of whales

PREDATOR
an animal that hunts other animals (prey) for food

PREY
an animal that a predator hunts and kills for food

REPTILES
a group of vertebrate animals that are cold-blooded, usually slither (such as snakes) or walk on short legs (such as turtles and lizards); generally covered with scales or bony plates

SEAWEED
group of algae that grows in the ocean

SHELLFISH
an invertebrate animal with a shell that lives in the water

SPECIES
a category, or kind, of animal or plant

SYMBIOSIS
relationship between two different species of animals in which each is helped by the other

VERTEBRATES
animals that have a spinal column, or backbone

ZOOPLANKTON
plankton made up of animals

BELUGA

CREDITS

CLOWNFISH

Abbreviations: GI: Getty Images; MP: Minden Pictures; NGC: National Geographic Creative; NGS: National Geographic Stock

Cover, Reinhard Dirscherl/Visuals Unlimited/GI; back cover (reef fish), Georgette Douwma/Photographer's Choice/GI; back cover (manatee), Brian Skerry; spine, Johannes Kornelius/Shutterstock; 1, Brian Skerry; 2–3, Flickr RF/GI; 4, Flip Nicklin/MP; 6 (LE), Fred Bavendam/MP; 6 (CTR), Doug Perrine/NPL/MP; 6 (UP), Reinhard Dirscherl/FLPA; 6 (LORT), Paul Nicklen/NGS; 7, Fred Bavendam/MP; 8 (UP), NASA; 8 (UPRT), Jurgen Freund/NPL/MP; 8, Beverly Joubert/NGS; 8 (LORT), Doug Perrine/NPL/MP; 9 (UP), Gary Bell/oceanwideimages.com; 9 (LO), Patricio Robles Gil/Sierra Madre/MP; 10–11, Fred Bavendam/MP; 12, Tom and Pat Leeson; 13, Fred Bavendam/MP; 14, Gerard Lacz/FLPA/MP; 14 (LOLE), Suzi Eszterhas/MP; 14 (LORT), Tom Mangelsen/naturepl.com; 15, Tom and Pat Leeson; 16, Mike Johnson/SeaPics.com; 17, Jani Bryson/E+/GI; 18, Patricio Robles Gil/Sierra Madre/MP; 19, Doc White/SeaPics.com; 20, Kevin Schafer/MP; 21 (UP), Peter Scoones/naturepl.com; 21 (LO), Michio Hoshino/MP; 22, Tim Laman/NGS; 23, Mauricio Handler/NGS; 24, Suzi Eszterhas/MP; 25, Frans Lanting/Frans Lanting Stock; 26, David Shale/naturepl.com; 27, David Shale/naturepl.com; 28, Alexander Mustard; 29, David Hall/seaphotos.com; 30, Fred Bavendam/MP; 31, Becca Saunders/Auscape/MP; 32 (UP), Sam Friederichs/National Geographic My Shot; 32 (LO), Pete Oxford/MP; 34, Favia Genus/naturepl.com; 34–35, Gary Bell/oceanwideimages.com; 35 (RT), Hiroya Minakuchi/MP; 36 (UP), Chris Newbert/MP; 36 (LO), Jurgen Freund/NPL/MP; 37 (UPLE), Chris Newbert/MP; 37 (UPRT), Sue Daly/NPL/MP; 37 (LOLE), Christian Ziegler/MP; 37 (LORT), Roberto Rinaldi/NPL/MP; 39, Fred Bavendam/MP; 40, Norbert Wu/MP; 41 (LE), David Fleetham/naturepl.com; 41 (RT), Chris Newbert/MP; 42, Brandon Cole; 43, Kathryn Jeffs/NPL/MP; 44 (UP), David Hall/seaphotos.com; 44 (LO), Hiroya Minakuchi/MP; 45, Gisele Rocha/National Geographic My Shot; 46, Roger Tidman/FLPA; 47 (UP), Michael & Patricia Fogden/MP; 47 (LO), Eric Baccega/NPL/MP; 48–49, Doug Perrine/NPL/MP; 50, Bill Harrigan/SeaPics.com; 51 (UP), Mark Conlin; 51 (LO), Robert F. Sisson/National Geographic/GI; 52, Brian Skerry; 53, Brian J. Skerry/NGS; 54, Brian J. Skerry/NGS; 55, David Fleetham/naturepl.com; 56, Mark Carwardine/naturepl.com; 57, Malcolm Schuyl/FLPA; 58 (LE), C & M Fallows/OceanwideImages.com; 58 (LO), Doug Perrine/naturepl.com; 59, Tony Heald/npl/MP; 60 (LE), Eric Wanders/Foto Natura/MP; 60 (RT), Wim Klomp/Foto Natura/MP; 61 (UP), Alex Mustard/2020VISION//naturepl.com; 61 (LO), Tui De Roy/MP; 61 (CTR), Mike Jones/FLPA; 62, Todd Pusser/npl/MP; 63 (LO), Doug Perrine/

NPL/MP; 63, Jim Abernethy/NGS; 64 (UP), Brandon Cole; 64 (LO), Flip Nicklin/MP; 65 (UPLE), Todd Pusser/npl/MP; 65 (UPRT), Richard Herrmann/MP; 65 (LOLE), Masa Ushioda/SeaPics.com; 65 (LORT), Alex Vogel/National Geographic My Shot; 66, Andrew J. Martinez/SeaPics.com; 67 (LO), Fred Bavendam/MP; 67 (UP), Jurgen Freund/naturepl.com/NaturePL; 68, Ingo Arndt/MP; 69 (UP), Flip Nicklin/MP; 69 (LO), Flip Nicklin/MP; 70, Kevin Schafer; 71, Konrad Wothe/MP; 71 (INSET), Colin Monteath/Hedgehog House/MP; 72, Frans Lanting/Frans Lanting Stock; 73, Andy Rouse/GI; 73 (UPRT), Kevin Schafer; 73 (LOLE), Kevin Schafer; 73 (LORT), Daisy Gilardini; 74, Robin Chittenden/NPL/MP; 75 (UP), Alex Mustard/naturepl.com/NaturePL; 75 (LO), Jasper Doest/Foto Natura/MP; 76, Doug Perrine/NPL/MP; 77, Jeff Rotman/NPL/MP; 78 (UP), Norbert Wu/MP; 78 (LOLE), Sue Daly/npl/MP; 78 (LORT), Jurgen Freund/NPL/MP; 79 (UPLE), Georgette Douwma/NPL/MP; 79 (LOLE), Sue Daly/NPL/MP; 79 (RT), Roberto Rinaldi/NPL/MP; 80, Reinhard Dirscherl/FLPA; 82, Carlos Eyles; 83, Alex Mustard/NPL/MP; 84, Doug Perrine/NPL/MP; 85 (LO), Ralph Lee Hopkins/NGC/GI; 85 (UP), Alex Mustard/NPL/MP; 86, Katsutoshi Ito/Nature Production/MP; 86 (INSET), Constantinos Petrinos/NPL/MP; 87, Claudio Contreras/NPL/MP; 88–89, Stuart Westmorland; 89, Jurgen Freund/naturepl.com/NaturePL; 90, James D. Watt/SeaPics.com; 91, Reinhard Dirscherl/FLPA; 92, Chris Newbert/MP; 93, Doug Perrine/NPL/MP; 94 (UP), Jeff Mauritzen; 94 (LO), Carr Clifton/MP; 95 (UPLE), Fred Bavendam/MP; 95 (UPRT), Scott Leslie/MP; 95 (LOLE), Fred Bavendam/MP; 95 (LORT), Alan James/npl/MP; 96, Mathieu FoulquiÈ/Biosphoto; 97 (RT), Georgette Douwma/NPL/MP; 97, Imagequestmarine; 98, Michael Patrick O'Neill/Photo Researchers RM/GI; 99, Michael Patrick O'Neill; 100 (UP), Philip Perry/FLPA; 100 (LORT), Beverly Joubert/NGC/GI; 100 (LOLE), Doug Perrine/npl/MP; 101, Claudio Contreras/NPL/MP; 102–103, Paul Nicklen/NGS; 104, Brandon Cole; 106 (UP), Doug Allan/naturepl.com/NaturePL; 106 (LO), Hiroya Minakuchi/MP; 107, Dafna Ben Nun/National Geographic My Shot; 108, Paul Nicklen/NGS; 109 (UP), Paul Nicklen/NGS; 109 (LO), Paul Nicklen/NGS; 110, Paul Nicklen/NGS; 111 (UP), Paul Nicklen/NGS; 111 (LO), Flip Nicklin/MP; 112, Paul Nicklen/NGS; 113, Paul Nicklen/NGS; 114, Paul Nicklen/NGS; 115 (UP), Paul Nicklen/NGS; 115 (LO), Paul Nicklen/NGS; 116, Michael Patrick O'Neill; 117, Andrey Nekrasov/VWPics; 118 (UP), Henry Jager/National Geographic My Shot; 118 (LO), Takao Otsuka/Nature Production/MP; 119 (UPLE), Mark Spencer/Auscape/MP; 119 (UPRT), Gloria Slaughter/National Geographic My Shot; 119 (LOLE), Pete Oxford/MP; 119 (LORT), Hiroya Minakuchi/MP; 121 Doug Perrine/naturepl.com; 122–123, Martin Walz; 124, Hiroya Minakuchi/MP; 125, Norbert Wu/MP; 126, Michael Gore/FLPA/MP

INDEX

Boldface indicates illustrations.

SEA OTTER

Prepared by the Book Division
Hector Sierra,
Senior Vice President and General Manager

Nancy Laties Feresten,
Senior Vice President, Kids Publishing and Media

Jennifer Emmett,
Vice President, Editorial Director, Children's Books

Eva Absher-Schantz,
Design Director, Kids Publishing and Media

Jay Sumner,
Director of Photography, Kids Publishing and Media

R. Gary Colbert,
Production Director

Jennifer A. Thornton,
Director of Managing Editorial

Staff for This Book
Robin Terry, *Project Manager*
Catherine D. Hughes, *Project Editor*
Eva Absher-Schantz, *Art Director*
Lori Epstein, *Senior Illustrations Editor*
Miriam Stein, *Illustrations Editor*
Stewart Bean, *Designer*
Sharon K. Thompson, *Researcher*
Ariane Szu-Tu, *Editorial Assistant*
Callie Broaddus, *Design Production Assistant*
Hillary Moloney, *Associate Photo Editor*
Carl Mehler, *Director of Maps*
Grace Hill, *Associate Managing Editor*
Joan Gossett, *Production Editor*
Lewis R. Bassford, *Production Manager*
Susan Borke, *Legal and Business Affairs*

Production Services
Phillip L. Schlosser, *Senior Vice President*
Chris Brown, *Vice President, NG Book Manufacturing*
George Bounelis, *Vice President, Production Services*
Darrick McRae, *Imaging Technician*

Dedicated to Ana, Allison, Avielle, Benjamin, Caroline, Catherine, Charlotte, Chase, Daniel, Dylan, Emilie, Grace, Jack, James, Jesse, Jessica, Josephine, Madeleine, Noah, and Olivia, the Sandy Hook Elementary School teachers and staff who bravely tried to protect them, and their loving families.
—CDH

A special thanks to Paula Keener, Marine Biologist and Director, Education Program, National Oceanic and Atmospheric Administration, Office of Ocean Exploration and Research. Her time and expertise were invaluable in the preparation of this book.

Acknowledgments
Jay Barlow, Ph.D., Southwest Fisheries Science Center, NOAA
Emma Harrison, Ph.D., Sea Turtle Conservancy
Denise Herzing, Ph.D., Wild Dolphin Project
Robert Rubin, Ph.D., Manta Trust
Guy Stevens, Manta Trust
Barbara Wienecke, Ph.D., Australian Antarctic Division
Georgia Aquarium, Atlanta, Georgia
John G. Shedd Aquarium, Chicago, Illinois
Monterey Bay Aquarium, Monterey, California
National Aquarium, Baltimore, Maryland
Thank you also to Jack Weible, Stephanie Hughes, and Blake Thompson for their support during the preparation of the book.

Since 1888, the National Geographic Society has funded more than 12,000 research, exploration, and preservation projects around the world. The Society receives funds from National Geographic Partners, LLC, funded in part by your purchase. A portion of the proceeds from this book supports this vital work. To learn more, visit www.natgeo.com/info.

NATIONAL GEOGRAPHIC and Yellow Border Design are trademarks of the National Geographic Society, used under license.

For more information, visit www.nationalgeographic.com, call 1-800-647-5463, or write to the following address:

National Geographic Partners
1145 17th Street N.W.
Washington, D.C. 20036-4688 U.S.A.

Visit us online at www.nationalgeographic.com/books

For librarians and teachers: www.ngchildrensbooks.org

More for kids from National Geographic: natgeokids.com

For information about special discounts for bulk purchases, please contact National Geographic Books Special Sales: specialsales@natgeo.com

For rights or permissions inquiries, please contact National Geographic Books Subsidiary Rights: bookrights@natgeo.com

ISBN: 978-1-4263-1368-4 (Hardcover)
ISBN: 978-1-4263-1369-1 (Reinforced Library Binding)

Printed in China

19/PPS/8